Harm.

NEW CALIFORNIA POETRY

EDITED BY	Robert Hass
	Calvin Bedient
	Brenda Hillman
	Forrest Gander

Harm.

Steve Willard

University of California Press   Berkeley   Los Angeles   London

University of California Press, one of the most distinguished
university presses in the United States, enriches lives around the
world by advancing scholarship in the humanities, social sciences,
and natural sciences. Its activities are supported by the UC Press
Foundation and by philanthropic contributions from individuals
and institutions. For more information, visit www.ucpress.edu.

University of California Press
Berkeley and Los Angeles, California

University of California Press, Ltd.
London, England

Library of Congress Cataloging-in-Publication Data

Willard, Steve, 1970–
    Harm. / Steve Willard.
        p. cm. — (New California poetry ; 19)
    ISBN: 978-0-520-24982-0 (cloth : alk. paper)
    ISBN: 978-0-520-24983-7 (pbk. : alk. paper)
    I. Title. II. Series.

PS3623.I574H37 2007
811'.6 — dc22   2006045593

Manufactured in Canada

16   15   14   13   12   11   10   09   08   07
10   9   8   7   6   5   4   3   2   1

The paper used in this publication meets the minimum require-
ments of ANSI/NISO Z39.48-1992 (R 1997) (*Permanence of Paper*).

Contents

Harm.

what little fountains we are

what with the differences nothing to be ashamed of

some of our fathers were perfumed spit out of the precious

mouth treasure at the bottom of a fountain neck

cocked back held by the red hair

•

My father condensed in the sky and was a lock who fell

from it. Dark feather you never clatter among that

tile array any louder than a smoke array upon it.

Only one compartment left to hold our sneakers

walked around the red tile like the town square.

•

dear ceiling of pierceable gold-color not to shine to rest

we throw victory our birth to the hollow air like breath

capped in the dark trunk of a tree by the changing climate:

a long way from the apartment holding the oboe's female

scent suffering not yet expanded us past the window even

so the window is open, there is no reason to make us a frieze of it

(Only Life . . .)

Extend the nets. A sifting breeze

  catch two hundred years singing must mean something
  and there is always easy anger to point the way flow.

  the glory of groves (movieesque or darking applejuice-

color of nets, oil-scratched sometimes (when the catch grows like a heavy breeze)

  a heavy breeze is the way a train moves. It makes those thinking of it
  in the cities, where a bristle is a bristle

  (in my frozen flower that palm of bristle is series of too many bright shadows)

to extend the nets—ecstasy is not arriving like
late framed steel-black—cannot hope really to catch it

      but must rally to separate the things seen including it.

Craftiquel Row (Side-Song)

Red raven, gloss of red

straying the face intercourseable

and excause

        over fabled chisel.

I carve what I can: day

    do red the top of a tree

        which is a side-boot

Raven of red engine yourself crawl

loving along the extinguisher-

angel furrowing the unplantable

      new trees

force that lies beneath diminishing

    branch after colour-like

    branch the intricate

    smallest seen peace.

Permission To Die

Figures come out, as darning, as an ash

down from the true clouds as in foil. If my own, skinnier voice there
were to hover in its lamphood and receive, replace
the colored readable wind . . .

Every minute isn't yet fully sleeping. Lace in the corner of things I didn't say passed
dusklike, like dusk
over a grate—flayed dusk-silk—,
over grated lining. (It had to have a link to the sun.)

Catching the silver-filtered contents as cardboard shapes covered (seeing like
a thought) in them, and are hunted among native mountains.
This ash tree left only the ability to do it; only foil or key missing in its leaves.
I hope it is a boat coming (but it is not)
that sound never observed.

With Slight Matter (Currents)

You create a month

     sometime into all the sap-lined traces between stone clouds

of the world an exemplary life closed-captions truth, standing, Standing

     under and to the side of: a red nylon banner blank lit

as much as it could want.

          In the air, to sense the drying, sticky heel

     tied in arrival: clear vein, well hidden, in a rounded clear,

                  keeping still

among us, and within itself . . .

       Closed life: raining down yourself as if one of your arms reaches

     or another's hand, leaf of green tree the passed through and stays on

        were going to help reach down the rungs of spine,

           yet remained across the leaf,

        falling past its coastal serrae from our sight,

    along the wanting to tell either of us that if it still exists,

       it is a more abstract quality:

     goodness maybe; maybe the sense and air to love the afternoon

How To Read "Harm" (This Book)

(eyebrows through chin) quick, as if a frame were lost;
a casket for _____ always was changing quick
"all," every owner and seller would want it to read, say)

and if it were a person sending metaphors thereof (being born
as if carefully chosen waves and is waved) (tiny rails in

as if what was occurring from Tuesday through Thursday
beginning to be pulled away toward some
but you were no person (as the water devours its dead)

divide being replaced—giotted water here (real water
dropped. Over the narrow sea each instrument like

First the cased viola from a wide railing
had been considered since the inception of the world. The world knows this

in the hail of notation, in a description of a sound in
it is not a dream where you devise the lionesque

it isn't a person. Tell one of us over the connection (step
the single apartment where the only livesoul hies) but

three fingers held faceclose and drawn down
toward the harpsichord (closed) and casket (open there

where concrete has been and still is. Can't view
yourself where the _____ begins and ends,

and an endless punishment becomes something else

your heart slides shy from as a difficult paragraph

without stopping since our situation was unlike this I gave

all help in a world imagined without stopping.

Continental Blue

caring pushes us just as a skin spoils,
"I have too much of the present to be shared by thee."

So success was put upon the earth like a handle or a stain
of the wooden present   I am run around by skin

and an apartment of flowing torches   flames are thumbs

(my mouth has a thousand thumbs in it)
             prospect of high cliffs choked with horn-wings

      backed up for miles from a seaboard

      (I shed my blood like an infant again and am a wing-array)
             again an infant stretched into the opposed life-array

And Being Imaginable

and some wonderment of sulpicient sign among
love's cessation held as they were holding an
assembly. Let the heavens solve forth in mice-
sounds and motion of calms and braidings of

what is heaven's and surely ours. Bait me
as guesswork among the wisest and beyond
other men. And if I can hold another man
or crowd of them along my tongue of plastic

hay and plastic dust threatening to produce
or part the feet as they thought merely to
describe the times and their relations where
we stood thought to nail thy staves and colors

Deliciae, Solaciolum

Pleated bird to me, pleated song and function
of bird, a sleephood filled just once into my remembrance
hangs in hands forever on the bow of this ship, a charm

preserving the world, a stilled part of her clock,
a few moments.

Touching yourself to me, pray as to God
the maps before you, a little bigger, and unsacrificed, than your face,
head siphoned as a spring, will be

three-dimensional, preserving the world
or his screens,

screen upon screen. The spring behind a pond pooled
of song. Can the grown girl saunter with her

basket, and cart away the mist appearing
as a mortal grid, screen upon screen, until

a nature, of neither this world or a next net's,
attends us, does not exist. That a face unlike
brushes, sails, beings and builds of altered paper

is bonded here, can't redip into this world paper

except as straddling the plane of each habit,

walls of a town liquid and in miniatures again,

as that cluster of note-like clear leaf-plates in the unturgid dream-air . . .

___less

stories and sorties upon which wonder down

    comes out of clouds handling the matter: why hadn't ever

        the monks, clear skin outside the chapel against their of-one-piece

robes (we would sew against the starholes lacekinds falling behind the times,

    times eaten away: thousands appear (days, years, starts) as of one fabric:

        (consumptions the fabric:

            why couldn't they sing the accompaniment to whatever before?

                (sometimes the accompaniment is a charmed machine.)

I want to enter heaven this instant but
these pineneedles come to cascading
a back of my neck—who has barely

touched it like temperatureless bright
sun, a non-hand on my neck unpainting

—tie air across my face, featureless understanding
to be full of pineseeds and tiny fists, tiny hearts,
woodlike, loamy buds within an eyelid air closing
to protect you I know you are there

Shingle Mirror, Average Bark

at the crucial juncture we meditate.:

    cool breeze expanded in summer come as over the pine mountains:
    over the blue-tinged hump or ridge,
    or just moved (not expanded)

    the white in the corner of my eye is a sealed towel. Your face is crying. I tie my
towel tightly (just not expanded)

    groundcover falling away from the square and perpendicular white—paint—
window (they would have, they knew the name of the cover)

    you imagine a people wriggling their law.

    the colors of my eyes ready the militia.

    "and you never see women you know."

Shadows (Numbers) Tell It (To The Executioner)

Man smell. Maybe proper grammar create
magnificent character, an ultimate character, a lane through

which the superior mouth, through which its silk-and-unable
to rest (even its inability) stood gleaming softly (visually)

(with loudness in nobility) half-through the musty
shadows. All (and at this word I would stop thinking you,)

        I can't total up effects generated in such

intimacies—no longer recognized of these.
And impossible remedy for as ulcerated air

breathed in by you would be to say the absurd thing from (the) beginning again.
        (I would have gone to my grave thinking.)

Board Of Rites

When suddenly all they fell open upon had disappeared
together. The sunset is of green-and-rice tea now: tea-colors.
Pale household, I'll think of you as I carry my suitcase along
on the prenight beach the colored-and-filtered tea kisses so

sweetly there is no thunking of a bass in this to hold us down.
Or if the sky sets itself of less and less dimmed tropical orange
out of your eyecorner elect single clouds on the color-threshold
of that other, spare, intense world ripples and wags without

wires, without time, without mercy from you, our cold spine,
letterless among queer and beautiful monstrosities.

Dial "O"

I stare into thy marching form
aligning thy painted bough
we'd flourish: they tire us
their normal innocences
apart running shy cosmetics
such disguises drawn on him
onward, lure me to mild weather

turn wonted from the clipping reality
up if by reference in wayfaring detail
as speeches reserving or resuming of
we are known to be averse and come
involute through which I have made
who is the very tail of man, corporating,
able to leap wide defects and therefore
let them live

Curved Glide Of Glazed Ambiguity

And the ghosts they gave up ordinary events

(which bore him

to leaflike water

were such that:

(fall flowers: (listing by   water

these tables   everything begot

fall these tables   a thousand velvet

petals

swatted past

ordinary tables

and as such   an I got delivered

(bore fall to the glass table's   lightly slanted   surfaces

between rains and our behaviour

call) occlusion   (and frost's let light)   homewardlike only the stares of fossils:

(a picture my curled-up-in-bed side)

inlet mist too bored to be wild,

and ghosts they gave.

(to walk now: among strangers. between inlet rains.   petal-surfaces thick
with

differents
(low or shallow   drain muscles,   who gave

(shells so something   a thousand leatherpetals thick,
without conquest
I could walk through
on my way among strangers

and they their ghosts
feet paddles
(reduction, really
would exist—

Heart Like A Drum

little wicked standard fondling ours through
the looking then

>   waste-person's in the hearth-baked
>   cooling street, little loaves smaller
>   then heavier than your feet,

>   swimming in: skinless pigs wine and chocolate
>   behind the glass, the shined teeming counter's
>   metal: but museum-makers in standard city

streets, you've avoided an age since then.

Immediately Thinking

toothless as salt: crimped rim. Overfed gateness.

A little leaflet of tears lilts, falls out. Garden

chewing on the stars and enclosed, the fissure

you're hearing sinks what you're hearing in the days,

toothless as salt. I guard you, I read

until I am carved.

•

a hole that rotates into a day thus largely I survive

apocryphal event and reason to hang her harp

through the convulvulus of an engine of our love:

that all dolls like ours be beaten, be written, be teared

away. I had produced no music. And the friends move on.

Old Hours

talked into relations it could still be there—an episode
there like a lamb. The curls are something when they arrive
instead of my skimpy reason toward loving you if one can aim
instead of being shot out of his own heart. I am off to the interior
of the pond worn from the cut-off fingers a-swimming in it,
not through it, as the paper bag you carry it in has the scenery
of our launch around it. Not since going anywhere when your heart
is a cube—occluded glass, plastic, or a cleared-out obsidion solid
paper. A paper cube and nothing existed to cut its sores . . . don't *abandon*
what you cannot feel—wait for it to assume *your* personality.

Bear And Policeman II: "Fairest, Lord Jesus"

The Damask. I left foundations foundering and amenning in stronger urges for which the climate-flower browses and turns unpiloted mystery. Too many hands shall last and dream at images, as a dream dies, at the opening-day.

Without Temperance.   That you have loved it of transparent scruff, brother, another ear and joy stripped of Samuel's Chinese Church might delight it. See the long and quick of goodly battlement downflowing your back's opening curlique, and if praise wake immobile hills let every wonder employ handling nature. Man raised from womb of leaves has risen in fleshy foils, so deftly the mind flays—

Charles Wesley.   be it ever so off of his dipping-stone, mild lays his mending. Out of noses, veritable, as milk, pour him, that sleepy foliage will not mind. Sing up, toys. . . .

The Damask. Recommending things stuffed into inconsumable tongs of golden hun, I purge the sop, I miss the sponges he'd lost out his wings, listen to a thistle who may not know a mountainside from the shoulders profiting slant out of old Europe. There is hope drooping and sawed to meet us. We care to dig ourselves in highest formations as are possible, out of the pictures there.

Wax Bay. No longer do proposals bind our hands with scented stems, as child may think. Concentrate the dedicate beeches as if the mountain were an opposite emblemate to sink, curse, dethorn certain clouds, certain as the dream expires its right to bloody wonders, by song, by employment, by ground-factor.

Charles Wesley. If I have peat I'd sing the glory postnation and to proof the whirling healing long, and vastly, dark as

at the bottom of death's laundry, glories streaming one after
another holy night until you're fairly—I think I interrupted to
the point of a blue squash ball emergent from my caption's
pocket. It was that night.

Temperance. Let all my characters clap a clod up on heaven-
born bending, a swallow its shapeless thunder. You inside
it listen: among heads set awry the souls' play sells people
forth from sleep. People soup! That's what I'd drink, given
a mouth. . . .

Without. If time breads into one Jerusalem and undying contents
the marble heightening without losing cloud shines
in passage with a spot. So a mood may surface and
survive that scene, commenting a chill. Strike us?

Charles Wesley. Soft drinks are the circular snows
gathering in your joy the starry mastiff calls remor-
se. What is that sheep-headed questioning hung
from mother's drying hall that single petals trans-
pose, now that dotted eternity is functioning like
a meadow.

A Damask. And all the imagination I can think of
winnows to no pole: wars may cease our crowning of
the sunshine and purer crags to rest and dry each fig-
like humour, only that moisted fabula can examine
in splendour its seemly tortuate. I heard it shriek.

The Iliad And The Odyssey

Some foreign country nobody knows
where freely, and without gifts their thoughts lean
and are strapped against a beech tree
and kill us.
See that closing, open light too often
suns from a high mountain, and flung it about the pens,

and the house falls in, with
the glare of its burning: some arrows left
between flakes of darkening, filling snow
invisible stand at height

a braided flush around these flakes

and casual transmittance of quiet to forelands
and heavens of gray sea:

your head is a fountain you have had no head

yet under reeds and thick brushwoodwork
night is counted

but the waves as they come rolling in unbanded stay
scrolled off a heart in the unbanded faggot snow

Dark Drop Hook

the air is crazy at night like a window in front of your head never so light to come

And to wander among blessed pill-shapes holding up the stem of a lamp: really it veins

combines grastling without mvt. in into the heat's. Waves of grain.

so warm I thundered

until the trace-lamp projected   now all times are cover.

a time we swell is definitive

Or collapses in into the throat. In the unpadded:

calling windows and

I apologize

I only apologize

the world is my
candle:

the world is   only the start
of a third argument.

Process Arquero

(back into thin oleanders

and in seeing the star some tortured snow spider

color   keyed out   of plum-shadows

the green oleander appetizers vinylized   or concrete

trust these dice floated whitely on their backs above fish

          are thrashless; the cubes turn

the clear-oil lamp in stars' own pattern

or patterns microphoned in leaves

leaning, into the light led black above

a thin wave, the sift-green candlehead's)

Candied Mai'nhood

I will now sing to please my quiver—
applechorus a-praying with victim-
stance that speeches us in heart and
stone secluded from views from the

main from the parallel cave. Bond
the buds together like torches in a
cup. Some troubles almost give us
ourselves in fuel consecrating hard

eroticism and frames, demands—I
will now sing to put out strict senses . . .

IV

Endures

Everyday Bostonians rise like onions to the sideboard life
and that's much more accurate that harvest falls like
bread shingles darkening from roof to allowed dirt

love hedges the floor. Gold letters "the compact edition"
in eider flowing (can't see, only intuit how the straw-
berries and square of baked crumblement arranged next)

you make a pepper float among paper air

a red head. Love's harvest is not letters: I was
among dirt like cassettes (how they flow from
an enclosure? so many gestures where efficiency

takes hold: everyone sniffs glue the same way
love is around that) and rigor rides like a cable
whose cargo is a view of each park, districts you,

needs red grapes and butter patterned like inturned
roses, you to let azure bloom and over your head.

Carmellathons

stand up carve your face into night like

capturing the old tree bark fallen to

the side walks with the side suns to

the relationship of wind-fed light to

tar one self to sleep. The sled is tar-

dark, the runners are pure sunlight rubber—

•

what forest demanding

if it is patrolled down

the clack-clear skinlike

bark (a waves' pressed

too close to merely shade

suspended track) (she is

taller than the frame)

still like water-shade

drottles, dry damps—

•

near uncaught by her

her its sourer hand.

But They Know

The other day I saw an in-line skater,

committing you to the grounds for your sins.
Being immobile, being human.

He made the pieces of the campus
hospitable ice. Passing over the (cool) green fields

and mud with a pepper shaker in his hand. Small holes. We put you
down and clasped your hands, the funeral was over and we all went outside to meet
the Florida sun. It was 5:30.

Not dark yet, but getting dark; the players hit flying
baseballs deeper
in the sky as the field within a circle of drainage rocks
below is given lines. It's a common theme, the capers.

—That we got ourselves into and surrounded by police. Pity

for the time held up under the metrorail on your bicycle, and A.,

mowed down by a firetruck on the other side of the world.

Why To Talk, What To Say

reasons, more than reasons,

in words before I reached for here:

broken stone- or broken razor-(edge) falling out (of grave depth, of miles of water
above us (and I asked the coming, "Are you the muse?"—wanting to bring you something
of yourself.—not possible)

and thinking that I am delivered my beginning to think again like the oversystem of
myself or that I recognized here,

a contradiction passing in "artificial" rain as between us only I was made by you
stepping into and out of it alone. These weeks: no thought of the untied symbol, a ring
floating in my hand like a red balloon the next morning, this had not refloated. Now,

and there nothere nothing of me in flight? Color fills between branches grey-beiged
like the side of a house—formerly I knew the space continued there beyond "possible"
vision.

And if (possible kindness: (another realm: my face that under a hard-beiged boot . . . face
an uneven, not battered, scuffed tin and roiled moon-surface: color directional, as my
head is taken from me each color seen changed into different, and some fewer, colors—
less drastic than (at) first assumed)

not housed (currently within: only seconds ago it was): question no. 1 I had of the form:
"if _____ is not your possible kindness (turned in me, toward my true self (is there such a
beast? what will he do? he should care . . .)), then what is it?" No more thoughts.

The stone or edge (metal) falling is either that, or pieces of cotton. (There is feeling.)
There is much to believe.

Stranded Voice/Deliciae

we have a significant shape
white cards out of hollowed barrels
caps turned over things we won

—in bound cards, the rainyday siren a drink in a cup held

(No horse stalks the white disappeared edges of a napkin

        (the wood is plush here

(eyes you disappear into her too)

Parking Timbre

the interior of my body is not separable
from the practices that make it visual,
that they light my bringing home of itself
refreshed after sleep as unaccustomed
to the missteps waking myself as I take
each, if it were wickedness to pattern
each clearing of porcelain dust's array after
my journey and the wet stone flags walked
it is cherry-blossom dust unfiltered
in leather pouches some construction holds
that thing tiring of tired wickedness: ambition:
I would drink your urine and have it (the
act) reflected, in sagebrush weather,
upon a knocked-on door: I will choose to drink
your urine, heretofore it tastes lemon-quiet

Cutting White Boxes

Slice a hand open like the (slice the bottom of the thick boat from
tip to pink wrist and bone-bracelets, rope-views, with leucine wash) only

unobservable surface of the thrown (like a falling wing-and-
body—arcs too good not to build summer-skater arcs as

summer's canvas lifted to the floor again from wind (I cannot keep opening
letters of those:

                    (the gallant child, thin as, all muscles slight
                    (and form remains touched
                    (where the adult adds tension throughout
                    (even selling sleep the settlements which so do not settle

          thrown: a vermillion bottle, a changing-fish   (rotates)

                    (but bereaved the arms with new veins worn, crayonic: tanfluid
                    (under the death-spots these arms of someone hold their
                    (pictorial weight.)

                and onto another cutting against amusement

                where in thread the first person (both of

                does not know amusement. Plans to laugh—

                            convincingly has laughed—

                            rotatingly at—

                            has design to stop the

convincing-laughter which certainly is not in him.

Butterfly Steak

So trees turn sick of me
but you have the patience
of a pearl

I believe the sail
and winds prosper as invisible
o'clock shadow

if there were our leaden trumpets
and you, desire of milk
pour or pout yourself upward to re-meet heaven's

V

(Crinkled)

then the light changed—outline a palm

so no more humanity to be written. I

speak no other tongue. That a blue lip

on the roof of Carlos V gas station has

cited up from rainyday surf's leading

a productive and peaceful divert down

through exploratory milk—you had to

sit quietly and I recognize (might order)

a pacific salad, a pacific spread—blue

lips rib you about the outpost where

plastic marlins stirred lipstick, Windex—

names from the other life had picked out

and interior apparel the latest walks quiet.

Not Ever = Not Now

Needed persons ministering to the happiness of a prince
or at a movement said or made peculiarly often without
any wicked purpose except the color of world changing—

notice: things within this room, like my handwriting—
some persons fail to understand the affairs on the corner
of dress undermining a stability of the night-blue parts

of the universe, which are in relief some

Ideas (Denuded)

A finger off the true song would be splendid equipment in this parlor

empty leggings from within a bowl of beige dust

line themselves flat into the cone and beige ardor of either God

in drenched circle of its room and returns of us:

(Or I didn't intend to know the human moleculus between their fold

between sand-numbed disturbances of dear afternoons

almost preferring a pure abstract wanting to know of song without

staring toward its point of utterance, for it fills the air

The Calm Repairs

scatter me up flatware, like an image
and death retired with a lock his kisses run
of roaches which is my ownest self in dark bracket

•

      sewn into white floor
      thy hand a thousand lithen candles)
      if love control such minds

•

you calm relenting stain alway white
sleep tied love shone

      (my breast a wood plate through
      quotidian fire thine endless were you

•

my heart is glowing with silly hearts. with cold surfaceless slide of inazure light

(so appraise my tattoo of stars nor thorns. as mercy blows price to the codewinds

(I vanish like a bath of tulle love work is the suckline fragment pulled off of me

and once you file down have you melt in the blood in thy heap thy excessive thy hay

(Invendavel)

Each hour fixed with plates (stars inside the coin's edge, five-pointed, repeated
a houseful of times and the house is in hundreds of thousands)

Each hour like a wig, and stop! (in a smock of battle behind the cloth door to you

•

Your cassock intoxicates you, you bronze inward. If only each day married the next. . . .

(But the home-born day swivels out of its association with these others

      so invendavel, inalienable, unsaleable,

and sends back letters to each apartment who is one minute short of his hour.

And sends the river letters back for itself, which self it lost writing itself—.

•

(You are master of no moment and also, you have gained no moment, no one.)

To Skystars, To Churchmouse

"Oh—so it's you I love—," I signaled to the churchmouse,

the cloud above nearly surprised as me, and it burst, purselike—

none of that rain reached us.

•

Scenes of incredible gratitude, the road to the house's walls cold as

as dead sod, in the season past evening and over the branchlike holding line

of night, but day isn't coming back again to redeem us.

•

So that none of the stars seem to fit the pieces of rectangular paper with its skystar

in mid-page and its sky pulled from that center, although each inhuman page is fading

into more a revealed hue more and more than human than its pure, opaque white self.

•

A year later: who knows what to make of me? Maybe always, in a dialogue perhaps

us or me and unseen sentences by a sapphire pool in a hotel atrium in Houston, TX—

only the plants here listening. Someone is coming for the pool; it's filled already . . .

•

—none too much after that episode I'm alone with my thoughts,

you understand when you watch the afternoon cross,

over a short steeple, bricks formed, painted white wood in form as well,

•

and more immediate the edge of the paved turnaround and parking spaces

and on the other side the field, on another plane of motion the timeless tracks

the train'll move on if there's later to be held, the quiet river, a green bridge

•

or two, one you'll walk on and one you can't. There's a dock and the calf-high grass

got marched to the edge of a river. If there's a hand in the music-box center to move

the lever that turns the wheel turning out the river almost constantly except today,

•

and which object or myself knows how long this field following a last afternoon

will last? Feel this way, lose the stories and misseeings which can color the afternoon

light and the still movie of stars in the sky, the lost stories say or will say

•

you're not a part of the world. What made us? I want to spend the dark alone less

than I ever have. There are clothes, freshly laundered, and white and denim

checking white, not steaming but lit up in that house-not-cottage the train passed

•

after running through the center of town all just six years ago. Movies showing

an endless depth of black and not-near flecked sky are always showing,

how many just now in the world? No harm I suppose in cataloguing all

•

the blueberry and cream croissants one walked back eating

from the store bridged over the tracks and chasm although

it feels to my now like a representative episode, eating once

•

and forever the best hand of food, only the memory of my morning ritual

keeps returning, on this, the one morning, before I entered.

There cannot be only one atrium with fronds I think of while walking,

●

there cannot be only one small creature with a heart worth signaling,

I have a few stories about other rats and mice, but what matters is what I can feel.

Today an unseen thing, which I must mention and do not name, is protecting me.

●

Today something else is setting out the boundaries.

Today something set the sea forth like a tablecloth and I'll visit it.

There's a minute never going to end containing all these and more—other beasts. Other

●

ideas. Other minutes than this very one.

Is There Anything Nugget Can Do?

Strawberry fender into the dust again no white side cart

the clear fair hair of the damned one (upon which no idea

falls: Brents everywhere repeating the one mantra known

about parts hidden from the sun: into the dark curve of metal

(like a street you let out like a cry (and believe I have been

locked close to the spiritually far (which I decorate from

•

Incoriant laughter; the rain is like soap and in this cold dark

of fieldsummer (made for you to open your eyes in) the sweet

dust that will become our countably endless sewn set of window-

curves opaqued to push substance out upon one world. Each

seed the standing row differently claimed if a slant has held

in many other than the old meaning; air following an airless

god to retain space in this field so the different standing views

all touched by the carrier of this (tan-in-the-air) conditioning

(rubbable skin) to be towed along.

Ed Palestrina

a fact which rises neither up nor down. Element
of thunder and electric lightless crossbar rambler
to capture a doorway and pass it by too. Soon we

were to write shades into the tortoise shells moving
love in a circle (can we let the pot stir) in extense of
troops' eyes—why you color. The coughing relieves

not quite as shadow-sound, that sound is forgotten
the way we make slaves sing. They are curtains
or letter-colors across the top of a thing, to hold it.

Where They'll Bury Me

Because there is no question that understands me like you understand me,
because quite outside differences of opinion there had been no way to teach
this world full of world anything of value, although it appeared for a time
that there were, and even then these artifacts and lost keys so easily findable,
as all I had to do was listen then, blocks of coral fettucine solving themselves
so that even to apply an effort to undo them seemed unnecessary. None of this
ever brought to the light by my bed anyone I love when I loved them, and it appears
now that you won't be stopping by much more, and even looking at me across less than
one human length of kitchen floor space as leaving occurs that will not close.
Walking in the woods or sitting by the whirring of a machine with you while
a human you were lets its violin play itself, I wonder that persons in this
can concern up with names of the specific leaves outside—to less easily drop
the life of that topic when touching your specific, beautiful neck, as you bent it
once and your whole self toward your knee, a picture of mirth welling from your
inner person, I happened to see this—it was not one of the chances to touch you
always so not with me, wherever I am.

Seven Pebbles

Stepped down from what path
as an anomaly in rain, inside

is it necessary, the subtended hearth,
and if one is fixed between

is it possible to step through rain,
even from above it. No contour other

than these pebbles has this succor
though our rain has dimension, is columned

unless the shoe lying flat in puddle
has no leg. A knowledge presented

as this has a definite end, even if we had
already left it.

____less

Each ____ is some flattened version of heaven

  so that all prove the version of some other particular for each particular looked

    upon and all are valuable, invaluable

      (one is removed many times from these things)

       (one is not one)

         (it was possible to feel the reverberance of the thing

        after all of the thing had itself removed

     reverberance which has always the same color of sound

   (which is that none living can see that color

  which is a slackening of the objections which lay claim to us.

(Ipsa Possem: Fragment

this world is, undisturbed except in the falling and falling

off of night as the puppet's head is turned.   the spine a sword again

where the filled well meets itself in   handle, the point of song

•

a sky is drenched, declined, if the laminated wood of deskness means

an afternoon above its speedboat blush of blue sky depressed

doubled dark the mirror that next time spring is pushed

down upon self, structured sprout (dawn, change of light, unbleached

elephantine surface of clothèd tree, no vine lunging from where

the _____'s mouth should have been; no picture of vine) (flat

      sketch of the way his or her arms project in an eternity:

•

To daub it in the readily spiced play of notes which could occur

to anyone, suddenly

•

wasn't dictated against the fact of yourself being here.
You are glowing within the forest as if you lay down your head.

Acknowledgments

Grateful acknowledgment is made to the editors of the publications in whose pages some of the poems in this book first appeared, as follows: *Colorado Review:* "The Iliad And The Odyssey"; *Volt:* "To Skystars, To Churchmouse," "Where They'll Bury Me"; *Boston Review:* "Immediately Thinking"; *Denver Quarterly:* "But They Know"; *1913: A Journal of Forms:* "___less," "Shingle Mirror, Average Bark," "Curved Glide Of Glazed Ambiguity"; *Wildlife:* "The Calm Repairs," "Cutting White Boxes," "How To Read 'Harm' (This Book)."

Text: 9/13 Adobe Garamond

Display: Adobe Garamond

and Trade Gothic Condensed

Designer: Sandy Drooker

Compositor: BookMatters, Berkeley

Printer and binder: Friesens Corporation